The Cherokee

Rennay Craats

AV² provides enriched content that supplements and complements this book. Weigl's AV² books strive to create inspired learning and engage young minds in a total learning experience.

Your AV² Media Enhanced books come alive with...

Audio
Listen to sections of the book read aloud.

Key Words
Study vocabulary, and complete a matching word activity.

Go to **www.av2books.com**, and enter this book's unique code.

Video
Watch informative video clips.

Quizzes
Test your knowledge.

BOOK CODE

H383934

Embedded Weblinks
Gain additional information for research.

Slide Show
View images and captions, and prepare a presentation.

AV² by Weigl brings you media enhanced books that support active learning.

Try This!
Complete activities and hands-on experiments.

... and much, much more!

Published by AV² by Weigl
350 5th Avenue, 59th Floor
New York, NY 10118

Websites: www.av2books.com   www.weigl.com

Library of Congress Cataloging-in-Publication Data
Craats, Rennay.
  The Cherokee / Rennay Craats.
    pages cm. -- (American Indian art and culture)
  Originally published: 2004.
  Includes bibliographical references and index.
  ISBN 978-1-4896-2906-7 (hard cover : alk. paper) -- ISBN 978-1-4896-2907-4 (soft cover : alk. paper) -- ISBN 978-1-4896-2908-1 (single user ebook) -- ISBN 978-1-4896-2909-8 (multi-user ebook)
  1. Cherokee Indians--History--Juvenile literature. 2. Cherokee Indians--Social life and customs--Juvenile literature. I. Title.
  E99.C5C76 2014
  975.004'97557--dc23
                              2014038975

Printed in the United States of America in Brainerd, Minnesota
1 2 3 4 5 6 7 8 9 18 17 16 15 14

122014
WEP051214

Project Coordinator: Heather Kissock
Art Director: Terry Paulhus

Every reasonable effort has been made to trace ownership and to obtain permission to reprint copyright material. The publishers would be pleased to have any errors or omissions brought to their attention so that they may be corrected in subsequent printings.

Weigl acknowledges Getty Images, Corbis, and Alamy as its primary image suppliers for this title.

Contents

The People

One thousand years ago, an American Indian group called the Cherokee lived in the southeastern United States. The meaning of the word *Cherokee* is not certain. Some people believe it comes from the Choctaw word *Tsalagi*, which means "people of the land of caves." Others believe it is from the Creek word *Tisolki*, which means "people of a different speech." The Cherokee called themselves *Ani-Yun'wiya*, which means "principal people."

The Cherokee moved north from the areas now known as Mexico and Texas to the Great Lakes region. Their territory covered eight states. They finally settled along the Tennessee River and stayed there for many generations. When European settlers arrived, they began settling along the edges of Cherokee land. The settlers and the Cherokee began to fight over the land.

CHEROKEE MAP

Location of routes traveled during the Trail of Tears

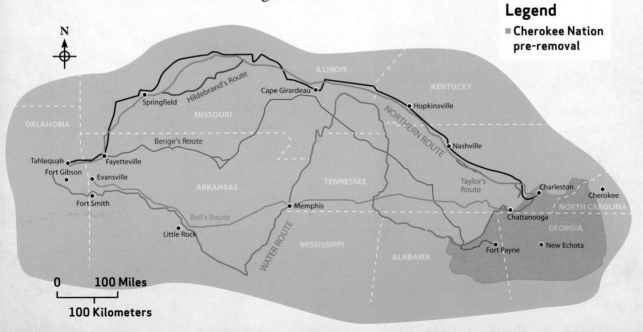

Legend
■ Cherokee Nation pre-removal

By the early 1800s, the United States government took control of the land. The United States Congress passed the Indian Removal Act in 1830. This act allowed U.S. troops to remove Cherokee peoples from their homes in Alabama, Georgia, Tennessee, and North Carolina. Between 1838 and 1839, about 16,000 Cherokee were made to march all the way to Oklahoma over rough **terrain**. This journey became known as the "Trail of Tears." Those Cherokee who survived the journey struggled to rebuild their lives.

The Cherokee lifestyle has undergone many changes over time. However, most Cherokee peoples combine their traditional ways with modern ways.

About 4,000 Cherokee died from disease and hunger along the Trail of Tears.

THE TRAIL OF TEARS

Before walking the Trail of Tears, **thousands** of **Cherokee** were forced into **prison camps**.

The **walk** to **Oklahoma** was **800** to **1,000** miles (1,287 to 1,609 kilometers).

The **Cherokee** were not allowed to take extra clothing, food, or blankets on the **Trail** of **Tears**.

Walking the **Trail** of **Tears** took between **104** and **189** days.

The **Cherokee** were allowed **600 wagons** and **carts**, **5,000** horses, and **100 oxen** for their journey.

Cherokee Homes

Traditionally, Cherokee **clans** lived in communities that were similar to European villages. Their homes were close together in rows that could be miles (km) long. There were usually 30 to 60 homes in a Cherokee village. Each Cherokee village had a town house. Ceremonies, celebrations, and political meetings were held in these public houses. Town houses were circular buildings. They were often built on top of dirt mounds. Benches were built along the inside walls of the building. The walls were made of woven tree branches that were covered with hardened mud. The building's roof was covered with tree bark to provide extra protection from rain and wind.

Cherokee homes were built around the town house. The households were large because many generations of families lived together.

DWELLING AND DECORATION

Town houses did not have windows. They only had a small opening for a door. Cherokee town houses were surrounded by a flat yard. Sheds built in the yard offered shade and shelter for villagers who gathered there for community events and special occasions.

Each household was made up of many buildings.

During the summer months, Cherokee peoples lived in large, rectangular houses made from **clapboard**. These houses were usually open buildings that did not have walls. They had grass roofs. Many Cherokee peoples spent most of the summer outside, so they did not need complex homes.

Cherokee Communities

Cherokee society is made up of seven clans. The clans are Bird, Blue, Deer, Longhair, Paint, Wild Potato, and Wolf. Cherokee peoples could not marry a person from their own clan. When two people married, they lived near the wife's family. This is because Cherokee society is **matrilineal**.

Traditional Cherokee society was also **democratic**. Every member of the clan helped make group decisions. Clan leaders could be men or women, and villages often had many leaders. By the early 19th century, the Cherokee began using some of the same governing concepts used by the United States. The Cherokee Nation created a **constitution** in 1827. At the same time, it created three branches of government.

Cherokee communities continue to work together to meet all the needs of their people.

The Principal Chief establishes laws and policies for the Cherokee Nation. A 15-member Tribal Council represents the districts of the nation. This council suggests **legislation** that affects the Cherokee peoples. Representatives on the council work as a team to improve life for the Cherokee. The Cherokee Constitution was revised in 1839 and again in 1976.

Teamwork has always been important to the Cherokee peoples. In the past, men, women, and children all helped tend to daily chores. Children helped to pick berries and collect wood for the fire. Older children watched over younger children, while the adults farmed, hunted, and worked. Often, women tended the fields, and men cleared the fields. Men also fished.

Cherokee family groups are close knit, with the older generation teaching traditional hunting and gathering techniques to youngsters.

COMMUNITY LIFE BEFORE 1838

By **1800,** more than **75%** of Cherokee had died from **diseases** such as **smallpox.**

By the **1820s,** the **Cherokee Nation** had its own **government, justice system,** and **police force.**

In **1835,** most **Cherokee** lived on **farms.** Farms were usually **14 acres** (5.6 hectares) of **cornfields** and **gardens.**

In **1832,** the **U.S. Supreme Court** ruled that the **Cherokee Nation** had the right to **govern itself.**

In the early **1830s,** about **25%** of all Cherokees could **read** and **write.**

Cherokee Clothing

In the past, the Cherokee did not wear many clothes. Deerskins were made into short skirts and shirts for both men and women. Children often did not wear any clothing when the weather was warm. During the winter months, deerskin cloaks and leather moccasins that laced up to the knees kept the Cherokee warm.

European settlers brought many types of clothing to the Cherokee. When the Cherokee were forced to leave their homes, families had to move away without their belongings and clothing. As a result, women did not have scissors to use for sewing. Instead, pieces of material were carefully torn from fabric and sewn into dresses.

These were called tear dresses. Tear dresses had three-quarter length sleeves and hung mid-calf, so they did not drag in the dirt. These traditional dresses are still worn.

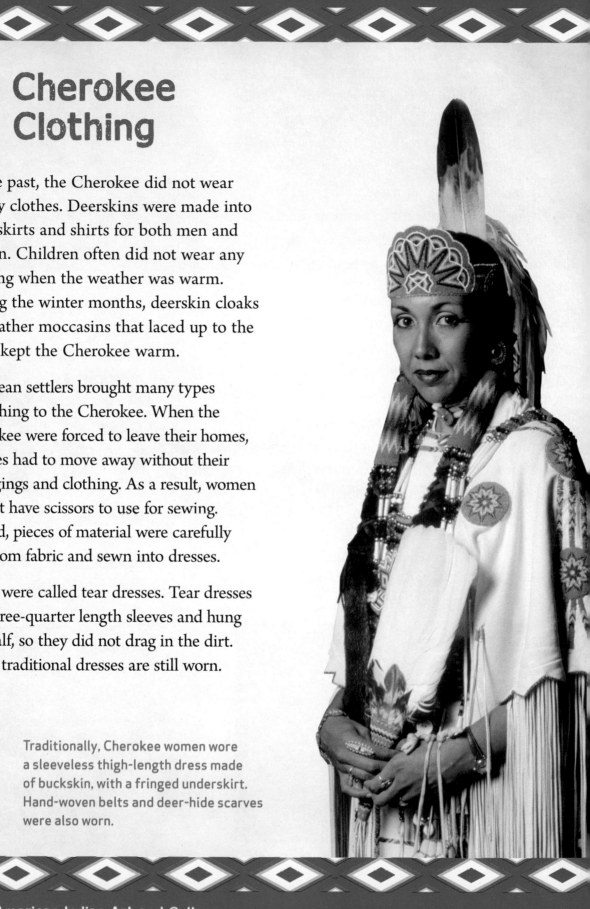

Traditionally, Cherokee women wore a sleeveless thigh-length dress made of buckskin, with a fringed underskirt. Hand-woven belts and deer-hide scarves were also worn.

The ribbon shirt is another traditional piece of Cherokee clothing. It became popular among other American Indian groups as well. This men's shirt was made with **calico** material. It had a ribbon design down the front and back. Ribbon shirts had three-quarter length sleeves that were similar to tear dress sleeves.

Today, the Cherokee combine traditional and modern clothes, such as jeans, with traditional belts or jewelry.

MODERN DRESS

Today, tear dresses are often made from calico printed fabric. They often have diamond, triangular, or circular patterns on them. Some feature the special seven-sided star of the Cherokee.

Present-day tear dresses are often worn with other layers.

Cherokee Food

Both men and women helped to feed the village. Men hunted wild animals, such as bears, deer, and elk. Women planted and tended the crops. **Agriculture** and cooking were chores for Cherokee women. Corn was a very important part of the Cherokee diet. It was used as an ingredient to create many different foods. Sometimes, the Cherokee ate fresh corn. Other times, they dried and ground corn into flour for making bread and other dishes.

Kanuchi is a **delicacy** among the Cherokee. Cooks prepared kanuchi by gathering hickory nuts, letting them dry, and then pounding them to form a paste. The paste was rolled into balls and boiled in water. The balls dissolved in the water and created a liquid as thick as cream. The liquid was then added to **hominy** and served hot as soup. Kanuchi is still prepared today.

Food preparation was important for the Cherokee's survival. It was also an important part of their social lives. Cooking for the clan brought women together.

Cherokee women grew crops of beans, corn, squash, and other vegetables. They added gathered foods such as roots, berries, seeds, nuts, and mushrooms to the meals they made.

Bean Bread

Ingredients:

- 1 cup cornmeal
- 1/2 cup flour
- 2 teaspoons baking powder
- 1 tablespoon sugar
- 2 cups milk
- 1/4 cup melted shortening
- 1 beaten egg
- 2 tablespoons honey
- 4 cups drained brown beans

Equipment:

- large bowl
- baking pan
- mixing spoon

Directions

1. Place all ingredients, except the beans, in the large bowl.
2. Thoroughly mix the ingredients.
3. Fold in beans.
4. Pour the mixture into a greased, heated pan.
5. Bake at 450° F for about 30 minutes, or until brown.

Tools, Weapons, and Defense

The Cherokee peoples were very resourceful. They collected minerals and wood, and used these materials to make tools. Quartz and other minerals were made into tools such as drills and scrapers. **Granite** was ground and polished to make axes and chisels. The Cherokee used wood to make traps for animals. Wood was also used to make valuable tools.

The canoe was an important tool the Cherokee used to travel. To make a canoe, the Cherokee cut down a yellow poplar tree, flattened the ends, and removed the branches. Then, they covered the log in red clay and set it on fire. Once the clay burned off, they chiseled away the charcoal. This process was repeated many times.

It could take up to several months to finish one canoe.

WAR AND HUNTING

The bow and arrow was an important tool. It was used to hunt large animals, such as deer. To make arrow points, the Cherokee sharpened pieces of bone, chipped flint, or stone. They used the same method to make spearheads, **tomahawks**, axes, and hammers. To make these weapons, the Cherokee used stones to sharpen and grind a groove around the edge of a bone or another stone. The Cherokee used **rawhide** to tie a handle to the groove.

Blowguns were used for both hunting and war. Darts were often poisoned with snake venom. Young boys learned to use blowguns before they began using a bow and arrow.

The Cherokee did not often begin wars. They fought to **avenge** the deaths of members of their group who had been killed by their enemies. The Cherokee believed the souls of the dead could not reach the Cherokee afterlife, called the "darkening land," until those responsible for their deaths were punished.

Between 20 and 40 warriors formed a war party. After killing the same number of people as the enemy had killed, the Cherokee **retreated**. Then, the enemy group avenged the loss of their killed members with another raid. War was an unending series of raids between nations.

The blowgun was used for hunting birds and small animals.

Cherokee Religion

Religion was an important part of Cherokee life. Religion kept balance and harmony. The Cherokee had great respect for the animal world. They farmed and hunted only to survive. The Cherokee performed rituals to apologize to the spirits of the animals they killed. They were so spiritual that material wealth held little importance. The Cherokee took care of both their people and the environment.

Medicine men and women were an important part of the Cherokee religion. They learned from the teachings of the medicine people from past generations. During healing ceremonies, drinking special mixtures or smoking tobacco was used as part of the medicine. This combination of ceremonies and substances was believed to cure the patient.

In Cherokee religion, humans and animals were closely linked. They believed animal souls also traveled to the "darkening land." These beliefs explain the respect and importance the Cherokee place in the natural world. Many Cherokee still practice their traditional beliefs, but today, some Cherokee also practice **Christian** beliefs. Changes have been made to traditional ceremonies, which are being performed less often. Still, many Cherokee peoples are working to **preserve** their culture.

Both in the past and today, medicine men and women treat both physical and spiritual problems.

CHEROKEE BELIEFS

The **owl, cougar,** and **cedar tree** are common **symbols** in the **Cherokee religion**.

The number **4** stands for the **4** directions, the **4** winds, and the **4 phases of the Moon.**

In the Cherokee **belief system, animals** had their own **town houses.**

According to Cherokee beliefs, *witches* could *trick a medicine person* into prescribing the wrong treatment.

The Cherokee believed in spiritual beings called **"little people."** If someone saw a little person, he or she did not speak of it for **7** years.

Ceremonies and Celebrations

The Cherokee held ceremonies and celebrations throughout the year. Many years ago, these ceremonies were performed in every Cherokee village. Today, they are practiced less often. Traditionally, there were six main festivals and religious ceremonies commonly held in Cherokee villages. Each ceremony involved **fasting** and feasting, dancing and music, ceremonial costumes, and cleansing rituals that purified the soul. Many Cherokee ceremonies were important because they called upon the spirits to help make their crops successful. During corn festivals, the Cherokee asked the Sun, the Moon, and the natural world to make the corn harvest plentiful.

Today, Cherokee take part in various ceremonies and festivals that celebrate their heritage.

The largest corn festival occurred when the corn crops ripened. It was called the Green Corn Ceremony. During this ceremony, villagers thoroughly cleaned their homes and town houses. They threw away all broken pottery, torn baskets, and any food left over from the previous year. Old fires were put out, and new ones were lit. All wrongdoings were forgiven.

The New Fire Ceremony was part of the spring festival. Seven people set out to create a new sacred fire. They used the inner bark of seven different types of trees. The bark was taken from the east side of the trees. Once the fire was lit, women took a flame from the fire and used it to relight their home fires. This fire symbolized the spirit of the Creator.

Ceremonies were held to maintain or restore balance and harmony within the villages.

HOLIDAY

Today, the Cherokee celebrate the Cherokee National Holiday. This day has been celebrated since 1953. The holiday recognizes the 1839 signing of the Cherokee Constitution. It is one of the biggest events in Oklahoma. Each Labor Day weekend, more than 100,000 people from around the world gather to meet new people, visit old friends, and participate in Cherokee activities.

The Cherokee National Holiday is celebrated in Tahlequah, Oklahoma. Visitors often attend local museums to see Cherokee displays.

Music and Dance

Cherokee ceremonies were filled with music and dancing. The Cherokee used music and dancing to pray and honor the spirits. Many Cherokee ceremonies featured rattles, drums, and noisemakers.

The Cherokee used gourds, pumpkins, and squashes to make rattles. The pulp of these vegetables was dried out. The seeds that remained inside would rattle when the vegetable was shaken. Musicians added pebbles or corn to make the rattling sound louder. The outside of the rattle was often decorated with paint or feathers.

Noisemakers were another common instrument. Cherokee musicians tied bones, sticks, or nuts together using string. They would shake the strings, causing these items to strike each other and produce sounds.

The Cherokee made instruments from natural materials they found around the village, such as rawhide, bark, gourds, and shells.

Today, Cherokee dancing and music are performed in competitions and displays.

CEREMONIAL DANCING

The Cherokee have a number of ceremonial dances, including the stomp dance. Stomp dance performers include a male dance leader, assistants, and at least one female shell shaker. Women are an important part of this ceremony. The shell shaker is the female partner of the dance singer leader.

The dance singer leader enters the sacred dance site. The shell shaker follows behind him, with tortoise shell rattles attached to her legs. Today, milk cans are sometimes used as stomp dance rattles. The stomp dance also includes sermons, feasts, and games.

The booger dance is another traditional Cherokee dance. This dance tells the story of the balance between the Cherokee and their environment. The dance is meant to protect the Cherokee by lessening the power other peoples have over them.

During the booger dance, the Cherokee often wear wooden booger masks. Some masks have aggressive expressions that are meant to represent enemy warriors.

Language and Storytelling

The Cherokee language was once spoken in every Cherokee home. Today, only about 20,000 people speak Cherokee. Fewer than five percent of young people are raised speaking the Cherokee language. However, Cherokee speakers are the seventh-largest group of native language speakers north of Mexico.

Cherokee is an Iroquoian language, which means it is similar to the language spoken by the Mohawk, Oneida, and Onondaga peoples. The Cherokee language is complicated. For instance, it does not contain the sounds made by the English language letters "b," "p," "f," or "v."

Language has always been an important part of the Cherokee culture. Traditionally, Cherokee storytellers, or myth keepers, could only tell their myths and tales to other Cherokee peoples or American Indians. Before attending the storytelling, a medicine person performed a **scratching ceremony** on invited guests. Then, storytellers would perform the stories. The storytelling lasted throughout the night.

Sequoyah wanted the Cherokee to be able to communicate even if they were far apart from each other.

Before 1821, the Cherokee did not have a written language. A Cherokee man named Sequoyah created an alphabet for the Cherokee language. He created a symbol for each sound or syllable. This was called the Cherokee syllabary. Using Sequoyah's syllabary, the Cherokee Nation created a written constitution in 1827, and published a newspaper, the *Cherokee Phoenix*, in 1828.

Cherokee Alphabet.

D o	R e	T i	Ꮼ o	O u	i v
S ga Ꮼ ka	F ge	Y gi	A go	J gu	E gv
Ꮚ ha	P he	Ꮟ hi	Ꮄ ho	Ꮽ hu	Ꮾ hv
W la	Ꮈ le	P li	G lo	M lu	Ꮣ lv
Ꮉ ma	Ꮊ me	H mi	Ꮱ mo	Y mu	
Ꮎ na t hna G nah	Ꭺ ne	Ꮵ ni	Z no	Ꮔ nu	Ꮕ nv
T qua	Ꮗ que	Ꮖ qui	V quo	Ꮘ quu	Ꮙ quv
U sa Ꭴ s	4 se	b si	Ꮬ so	Ꮤ su	R sv
Ꮶ da W ta	S de Ꮦ te	Ꮦ di Ꮧ ti	V do	S du	Ꮯ dv
Ꮰ dla Ꮮ tla	L tle	C tli	Ꮴ tlo	Ꮕ tlu	P tlv
G tsa	V tse	Ꮳ tsi	K tso	J tsu	C tsv
G wa	Ꮿ we	Ꮺ wi	Ꮼ wo	Ꮕ wu	6 wv
Ꮿ ya	B ye	Ꮏ yi	Ꮷ yo	Ꮹ yu	B yv

Sequoyah's table of characters to represent the Cherokee language was approved by Cherokee chiefs. Within a short time, thousands of Cherokee learned to read and write.

STORIES

Cherokee stories have been passed down through many generations. Storytelling is an art form. Storytellers are actors, singers, dancers, and mimes who tell stories about the Cherokee people and animals. Animals are important in Cherokee stories. Many stories tell of people who could speak with the animals. Some stories tell how the Cherokee could once communicate with animals. According to this belief, the Cherokee lost this ability because their ancestors were greedy and talked too much.

Cherokee Art

The Cherokee began making arts and crafts out of necessity. Most items they made were objects they used every day, such as baskets to hold corn or masks that were worn during ceremonies. Over time, these everyday items came to be recognized as beautiful pieces of art. There are many kinds of arts and crafts made by the Cherokee.

Cherokee basketmaking dates back to ancient times. Cane was the most common material used to weave baskets. Baskets were made with two layers of weaving. This made the baskets very strong and useful. To decorate their baskets, Cherokee women made dyes out of such plants as bloodroot, walnut, and butternut.

Traditional basketmaking is rarely practiced today. However, some Cherokee women still make baskets using commercial materials.

Cherokee women made pottery using only clay and their hands. They rolled the clay into long ropes and coiled them around to make pots. Potters used stones to smooth the pot and to carve designs into the piece.

Cherokee potters often stamped geometric symbols into the clay. Once the potter finished shaping the piece, it was set aside to dry. Once dry, the pot was baked in hot coals. The type of wood used to fuel the fire determined the color of the pot. The Cherokee often added dried corncobs to the fire to make black smoke. The hardened finished product was unglazed and black.

The Cherokee also made special belts with shell beads woven into them. These were called wampum belts. Wampum belts held meaning and messages.

Another pottery-making method involved pushing one's thumb into the clay to mold it into a desired shape.

JEWELRY AND DECORATION

The Cherokee believe the **corn crops cried** and **drooped** as the Cherokee walked the **Trail of Tears.** Cherokee women made the corn's **teardrops** into necklaces of cornbeads.

The **"Cherokee Rose"** is also a popular symbol in Cherokee jewelry. There is a story that **roses** grew where Cherokee women cried along the **Trail of Tears**.

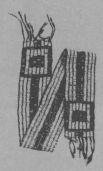

Wampum belts were exchanged at **meetings** and during **official business**.

Some Cherokee **wampum** belts feature woven **words** from the Christian **Bible**.

 Stickball

Cherokee communities played many games. One game they played was stickball. Stickball built skill and **endurance**. The Cherokee used stickball to train young men for battle and to settle disagreements between groups. Stickball was sometimes called the "little brother of war."

A stickball game could last for days. The game was played on a large field. Stickball players carried two sticks each with a basket on one end. Players used the basket to catch and throw the ball. They had to hit goals, which were often a tree or rock, with the deerskin ball.

There were usually about 100 stickball players on each team.

There were no rules to follow in a stickball game. Players did not wear any protective clothing. There were often many injuries, and a player could die during a game of stickball.

For many American Indians, stickball games were used to recreate the story of creation, in which there was a battle between good and evil. It was even played to honor the dead, cure the sick, and to bring good weather.

A version of stickball is played today as a competitive sport. It is called lacrosse.

CHEREKEE GAMES

Stickball was temporarily **outlawed** by the U.S. government in the **early 1800s** for being **too violent.**

In the past, **medicine men blessed** their stickball team. They also placed **curses** on the opposing team.

Stickball is still played throughout the Cherokee Nation. Players try to hit a **wooden fish** at the top of a **25-foot** (7.62-meter) pole.

The Cherokee also enjoyed a game called **Chunkey.** Disc-shaped **stones** were rolled, then **spears** were thrown as close as possible to the stones.

Chunkey was played in **huge 47-acre** (19-hectare) **arenas** with large audiences.

STUDYING THE CHEROKEE'S PAST

Archaeologists and **anthropologists** have learned a great deal about the early Cherokee. They estimate that the Cherokee first appeared between A.D. 1000 and A.D. 1500. This is 500 years before the first Europeans came to North America. Scientists believe that a group called the Pisgah are the Cherokee's ancestors. Archaeologists have discovered villages, tools, and **artifacts** belonging to the Pisgah. These Pisgah items are very similar to the items made by the Cherokee. From these items, scientists were able to determine that the early Cherokee ate animals, nuts, fruits, and seeds.

The dirt mounds archaeologists found in Pisgah villages are clues to the types of ceremonial and political practices of these communities.

Timeline

Cherokee Written Language Established

1821—1827

The Cherokee syllabary was completed in 1821. The first written law was created in 1824. In 1827, the Cherokee Constitution came into effect.

Removal and Resettlement

1838—1866

From 1838 to 1839, about 16,000 Cherokee were forced to walk the Trail of Tears to Oklahoma. From 1865 to 1866, the Cherokee negotiated peace with the U.S. government. A new treaty limited group land rights.

European Settlement

1838—1866

Unassigned land in the Indian Territory was opened to European settlers.

The first written records mentioning the Cherokee appeared in the 1500s. These records did not explain Cherokee culture. The records described the politics of the group and its relationship with its neighbors. By the mid-1600s, more detailed reports about the Cherokee began to emerge. Traders and travelers often wrote about them.

By studying artifacts such as arrowheads, archaeologists can learn more about a people and their history.

Indian Reorganization Act

1934

The Indian Reorganization Act created a land base for American Indian groups and a structure for self-government.

Cherokee Nation Government

1948—1987

The Cherokee Convention was held in 1948, and the Cherokee Nation government was reformed. In 1976, the Cherokee Constitution was updated. Wilma Mankiller became the first female elected chief in 1987.

Modern Cherokee Nation

Today

The Cherokee Nation has more than 317,000 citizens. The Nation operates courts, businesses, and services.

QUIZ

1 How many Cherokee were forced to walk the Trail of Tears?

A. About 16,000

2 Traditionally, how many homes were there usually in a Cherokee village?

A. 30 to 60

3 Cherokee society was made up of how many clans?

A. Seven

4 What year did the Cherokee Nation create a constitution?

A. 1827

5 Which unique style of Cherokee clothing is said to have come about as a result of the Cherokee being forced to leave their homes?

A. Tear dresses

6 Which food made from hickory nuts is a delicacy among the Cherokee?

A. Kanuchi

7 Which Cherokee tool was used for both hunting and war?

A. Blowguns

8 Who were the ancestors of the Cherokee?

A. The Pisgah

9 What was a popular game traditionally played in Cherokee communities?

A. Stickball

10 How many main festivals and religious ceremonies were commonly held in Cherokee villages?

A. Six

KEY WORDS

agriculture: raising livestock and producing crops

anthropologists: scientists who study human origins, development, customs, and beliefs

archaeologists: scientists who study objects from the past to learn about past civilizations

artifacts: objects used or made by humans long ago

avenge: to repay with an attack or injury

calico: multi-colored, printed cotton fabric

Christian: a belief system based on the teachings of Jesus Christ

clans: groups of people who are related

clapboard: a long, narrow board that has one thicker edge

constitution: a written document that includes the rules by which a group is to be governed

delicacy: a special food

democratic: a system of government in which the entire population of a society elects its leaders

endurance: the ability to do something for a long period of time

fasting: going without food, often as part of a religious or political ritual

granite: a very hard gray, pink, and black rock

hominy: dried corn that is boiled

legislation: the process of making laws

matrilineal: kinship that is traced through the mother's lines

preserve: to keep safe

rawhide: untanned hide

retreated: withdrew or pulled out of a battle

scratching ceremony: a ceremony in which a medicine person scratches a guest's arms with a comb made from rattlesnake teeth, then blows a healing powder over the scratches

terrain: the surface features of a piece of land

tomahawks: lightweight axes

INDEX

Log on to www.av2books.com

AV² by Weigl brings you media enhanced books that support active learning. Go to www.av2books.com, and enter the special code found on page 2 of this book. You will gain access to enriched and enhanced content that supplements and complements this book. Content includes video, audio, weblinks, quizzes, a slide show, and activities.

AV² Online Navigation

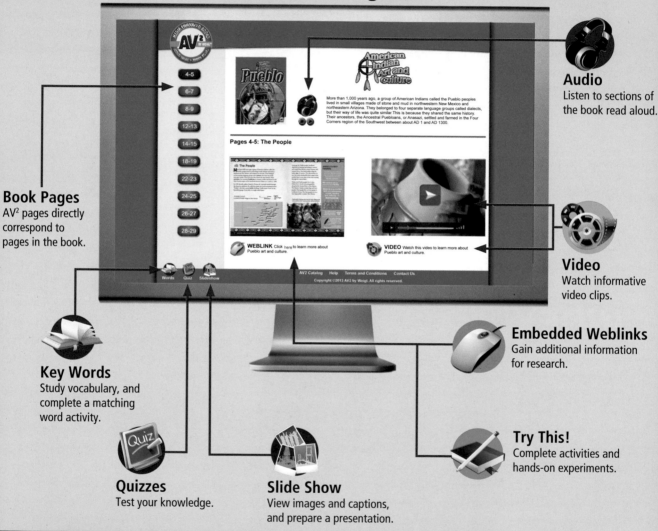

Book Pages
AV² pages directly correspond to pages in the book.

Audio
Listen to sections of the book read aloud.

Video
Watch informative video clips.

Key Words
Study vocabulary, and complete a matching word activity.

Embedded Weblinks
Gain additional information for research.

Try This!
Complete activities and hands-on experiments.

Quizzes
Test your knowledge.

Slide Show
View images and captions, and prepare a presentation.

AV² was built to bridge the gap between print and digital. We encourage you to tell us what you like and what you want to see in the future.

Sign up to be an AV² Ambassador at www.av2books.com/ambassador.

Due to the dynamic nature of the Internet, some of the URLs and activities provided as part of AV² by Weigl may have changed or ceased to exist. AV² by Weigl accepts no responsibility for any such changes. All media enhanced books are regularly monitored to update addresses and sites in a timely manner. Contact AV² by Weigl at 1-866-649-3445 or av2books@weigl.com with any questions, comments, or feedback.